Confession of a Heliophiliac

Poems by

Rochelle Germond

for Jerred

Table of Contents

The Problem with Moving to Raleigh

I.

There are no lizards here. No
lidless eyes to follow the gait
of a spider across the eggshell-painted wall,
keeping his distance with
well-placed webbed toes, lapping up
his meal with a tongue swift and precise.

II.

There are no lightning storms, the rainless,
thunderless kind created with only the silent
heat of August midnights, the kind that leave
nothing but neon flickering
behind closed eyes, like the glow
of a bar's OPEN sign.

III.

I have no central air. My studio apartment
is cooled and heated by the machine
under my window. It cycles on
and off, gurgling water, recirculating
the air that I have been breathing for months,
air that smells like a hotel room,
an unpacked suitcase, a bed slept in
by someone only passing through.

Somewhere North

Sometimes, late at night,
when I'm on the interstate driving
to you, I follow the semis, close enough
so no other car can come between. Seventy
miles per hour feels too fast with all that black
squeezing my small sedan, so I go sixty, tucked
behind mudflaps and tires. Vehicles pass me,

other semis, their silver rears reflecting my headlights.
Shiny hineys, my dad would call them
when I was little. He and my mom used to drive
across the country in a semi, quitting
after five years because my mom wanted
her own bathroom. She told me once

that they waited so long to have kids
because my dad wasn't ready. But I found a book
in the den titled "How To Repair Your Relationship"
with an inscription from my aunt dated three years
before I was born: *you'll make it through this.*

Sometimes I wonder what it will be that almost ends us.
If it'll be the toaster oven, or the fitted sheets, the water
left pooling on the counter by the sink, the books
stacked under the window, a concert, a broken
keychain. I wonder if it'll be our differences, how I believe
in fate and the importance of the things we say,
how you think love is just a pulse in a vein,
that a poem is just words on a page.

Gram's House

You kept the grocery bags in the hall closet,
folded next to the monkey
made of socks and buttons
and the Cabbage Patch Kid with knotted yarn
hair the color of your pumpkin pie.

I scribbled my future onto those brown paper sacks
that once carried cans from Wegman's
to your kitchen cupboards. They were the blueprints
for my dreams: a two-story house
with a Christmas tree in the window, unashamed
of its decorated body, its lit boughs.

You and Mom sat nearby while I sketched,
the lifted table leaves holding cups of coffee,
your lilting voices holding whispers of things
like heart disease and trial separation,
abnormal cells and accidental conception,
the ways people hurt one another,
the ways that we are torn apart.

Sprawled at your feet, stomach against the cool
hardwood, my crayons were all that mattered.
Printed with names like bubblegum and denim,
bittersweet and raw umber, all scattered
on the thin floor rug beside me, its faded
roses covered by my young colors.

You kept those grocery bags in the hall
closet, before you moved to the condo
by the lake, before Wegman's switched
to plastic, before the Cabbage Patch Kid
lost his yarn and the monkey's button
eye fell off, before you threw them away.

Things I Didn't Know I Loved

after Nazim Hikmet

I didn't know I loved
the smack of the screen
against the splintered frame
as you moved from the house
to your workshed out back
on Saturday mornings,
the front door flung wide
to welcome the mosquitoes.
I didn't know I loved

the humidity, curling my hair
back to its natural state, soaking
the soles of my feet.
I didn't know I loved

the way you speak
in sleep, the mumbled fragments
of dream dialogue, phrases tumbling,
colliding into each other like bumper
cars at the fair. And the bathroom mirror
splattered with dried water spots, specks
of toothpaste dotting the sink's
porcelain edge. I've always

loved the sand sugaring
the cushions in my car,
salting my skin, impossible
to scrub away. But I didn't know
I loved the heat, melting mirages
above flat streets. And trains,
the hourly whistle I can hear
from the kitchen in my third floor
apartment, the ticking tracks counting
miles as minutes. And here I've loved your eyes

all this time, but I didn't know
I loved the freckle on the inner rim of your left
eye, where the skin is always moist,
like the underbelly of a frog. I want to kiss you
there, read the raised dot with my lips
like Braille. I remember the rain,
how I love that too, the thunderstorms
every August afternoon at four, the mist
in the mornings of Florida
winter, the drizzle that seeps
through layered clothes, replaces
marrow with its breath. But I didn't know

I loved the rain that stops suddenly,
leaving acrid asphalt in my nose
and katydids calling in the damp
sunlight, shocked into song.

Hunger

Some nights, I want to eat everything:
the cheese slowly molding in my refrigerator drawer,
linguine, raw and in fistfuls, scoops of margarine
out of the plastic tub. I want to open up the dusty cans
of French style green beans and sweet baby peas
in my cupboards, the chicken noodle soup
and apple pie filling and gorge myself on them,
cold, straight from the tins. I would devour
the whole world, rivers laden with trout and salmon,
fields of corn, cranberry bogs, trees dripping peaches,
nectarines, cherries. I'd fill my mouth with stars

like cookies covered in sugar, bite through
the rings of planets, savoring their cinnamon and ginger
crumbles before moving on to the planets themselves,
twisting them apart to find cream-filled centers, licking clean
their wafer husks. I want to nibble the Milky Way
like a raspberry, black holes like the liqueur-soaked
lady fingers of tiramisu. I want to swirl the heavens' dust
on my taste buds, sweet and salty like chocolate-covered pretzels,
trail mix, kettle corn, this star stuff we are made of,
this billion-year-old carbon, these ancient elements I can taste
when my tongue meets your skin.

Long Distance Relationship

Now that you're gone, I sleep
in the middle of the bed, my head
swallowed by the crease
where the pillows meet. I eat
the whole dessert, or none at all,
ignore the buy-one-get-one-free
deal on Publix ice cream when I go
to pick up dinner for one.

Now that you're gone, I use your soap
in the shower. I have long since run out
of my own shampoo and conditioner,
the rose-scented body wash I never
bothered to replace. My razor slides
through your shaving cream, scraping
the stubble that has sprouted
since we last slept in my double bed.

Now that you're gone, I paint
my toenails Chapel of Love – pink,
the color of the bows on the girl's
dress, of the petals she drops over the white
canvas. *If I had been the ringbearer,
and you had been the flower girl*, you say
in a tone so low I have to watch
your lips move to make out
the words, *I would have just given you
the ring instead.*

The Bermuda High

*Year after year, hurricanes are shuffled west along
the southern edge of the Bermuda High,
a massive high-pressure zone over the Atlantic
that forces storms toward the tropical
waters of the Gulf of Mexico.*

I.

There are hundreds of spaghetti models for Irma,
a chaos of thin lines that criss-cross the state
and make it impossible to tell where Florida begins or ends.
The most common one has her traveling straight up our spine,
splitting us in half with her well-formed eye, stretching
her outer bands so wide that she covers us
from shore to shore, panhandle to peninsula tip.

II.

I left my hometown on the Gulf coast of Florida five years ago
and now live hundreds of miles and three states to the northeast
in a city whose hockey team is named after this storm
I've come to fear the most. I ask my parents to evacuate,
come stay with me for a week or two, but my dad is stubborn
and my mom is loyal, so they board up their windows and wait.

III.

Even when the storm is christened and reclassified
as a Category 1, then 2 and 3, locals are preparing to stay–
to *ride 'er out* and *hunker down* and *drink 'til it's over.*
They are spreading the word about hurricane parties,
stocking up on beer and booze, essentials
deemed the most crucial to survival.

IV.

Legend has it that the city of Sarasota is protected
from hurricanes by an ancient Native American blessing,
put in place by the tribes who roamed the region centuries ago.
Growing up, we all thought it was true, this urban myth
that was handed down and passed along, bolstered by the fact
that our town had not been the target of a major storm
since at least 1871, when reliable records began.

V.

It's not until the traffic on I-75 is described as a parking lot
and gas tankers are no longer refueling stations,
leaving pumps dry from the Keys to the capital,
not until Irma is a Category 5 – *complete destruction*
of homes, shopping centers; trees uprooted,
extreme flooding; area uninhabitable for weeks
or months – and Fox 13's Paul Dellegatto is doing his best
to keep thousands of viewers calm, but his updates come
every few minutes now instead of every few days,
it's not until the store shelves are raided, wiped bare
though the lines still wrap around themselves twice
in front of local Publixes and Home Depots,
it's not until flights are grounded or going for thousands
per seat and no one is planning hurricane parties anymore
that we all realize how bad this will be,
when even the old-timers, who survived Donna in 1960
and haven't left the state since, are getting the hell out.

VI.

Hurricanes wreak havoc in my sleep. I dream of water
seeping into refrigerators, stealing away food
no seasoned Floridian would stock in preparation
for a storm: slices of lunchmeat and cheese,
orange juice, eggs, mayonnaise. I see pines falling
into my childhood home, pinning my parents inside,
me, powerless in Raleigh, them with no way to escape.

VII.

I'm at the mall in Raleigh the Saturday Irma makes landfall
just south of where I was born. No one around me is alarmed,
not the moms pushing sleeping babies in strollers
or the clusters of teenagers hanging out in the food court,
not the cashier at Bath & Body Works who rings up my candles
and pumpkin-scented soaps, smiles and tells me to have a nice day.
There's a hurricane coming for us I want to scream
it's going to take everything, it's going to take everyone we love.

VIII.

Weeks later, my mom tells me she still feels stressed,
says she must be going crazy. But I've read the articles
about out-of-whack adrenal glands and symptoms of PTSD
in storm survivors, the possibility of developing depression
in the wake of a hurricane, even if you haven't suffered
tangible loss, even if you can consider yourself lucky.

IX.

It wasn't famous folklore or sacred ground that saved us
from Irma, but a matter of miles, a slight shift in the storm's course
at the last second, a collision between a trough of dry,
low-pressure air and the western edge of the Bermuda High
that caused Irma to wobble, pushing her just far enough to the east.

X.

My mom calls the morning after the hurricane has passed
as she and my dad make their way back home
from the church they evacuated to. I ask her how it looks
and she starts to cry, she whispers *My house is okay,*
oh my God, it's okay, it's okay, we're okay.

She describes the intact roof shingles and vinyl siding,
the lanai screen that has gone unscathed,
the Christmas cactus sitting untouched in its planter
just outside the sliding glass doors, the shed in the side yard
the only damage, its plastic frame dented
by a fallen limb.

Playing House

The floral-printed cotton is held up
by clothespins and chairs, like it was
when I was young and would spend my days
playing house. Our backs against my Persian rug,

we try to form shapes from the billows and pleats
above us, as though they're the wisps in the sky,
as though there isn't a thunderstorm whooshing
away any light outside. You say you see

a dragon, fire spewing from his mouth,
and a princess, needing to be rescued.
I say I see babies, like the ones
we could have had. I can still feel them

beneath me where they fell
hours earlier, trickling down my thighs
after you pulled away, penetrating the fibers
of the carpet, getting lost in the dark
naves of the flowers there. The damp
paper towel you brought back
from the kitchen couldn't save them:

the Chloes with my gold-sharded green
eyes, the Jacobs with your mouth,
the parentheses that punctuate your skin
when you smile. I see them now, in those

linen clouds, and I want to know how
we get them back, I want to know
how, in the tangle of arms and legs and hands,
we forgot them.

Missing

Some days I don't speak at all. It's not that I don't want to,
but there's no one to talk to in my studio apartment on Thursday
through Monday, when I have no reason to leave. Sometimes
I wonder what would happen if it were this way every day.
People might ask about me for a little while, sure,
but in this city of acquaintances, my absence wouldn't warrant
a segment on the evening news. A few weeks ago, I read a story

about a woman who hoarded cats. She collected them
like some collect stamps, like I used to collect teddy bears
when I was in elementary school. I named them,
counted them each night before bed to make sure
they were all still there. I figured this cat lady did the same.

Animal services searched her house when they found out
about the cats, discovered carcasses in the crannies of rooms
she never used. She had forgotten, she said,
how many she had, lost track of some, had given up
the search for the ones she thought were missing for good.

Seasonal Affective Disorder

It's the time of year when the outside air sneaks in
through the unsealed windows and settles
on every surface, in every pore of the hardwood floor,
when the days clump together just like the clouds do,
gray and thick, the same weight as the blanket I dig out
from the cedar chest in the corner of my closet,

when even if there were any sun, it would only last for a few hours,
in between the morning dark and the dark that forces me
to turn on my lamps before five each evening,
even earlier if it's dull out, or if I'm feeling glum,

both of which are usually the case. I should find
one of those light boxes like they sometimes have in clinics
and in therapists' offices, with a name like the Happy Light
or Lightphoria. I could sit in front of it for thirty minutes every day,

to counteract the symptoms of this season, the bulb acting
as my sun, administering my daily dose of warmth
and happiness. In Europe they sell light-emitting earbuds,

the brightness moving through cochlear hair cells
to reach synaptic ribbons in the brain. Twelve minutes a day
and even "psychologically healthy" volunteers
showed an overall improved mood.

Instead, I sit in my sweats and pop more vitamin D
than the bottle suggests, eat tropical fruit from a can
and wish I were the leaves on the maple tree outside
my kitchen window, there one morning but missing

the next, gone to rest on the hoods of cars, in rain gutters
and wheels of grocery store shopping carts,
in the train tracks that run from here to Florida.

The Red Line

We ride the color-coded lines all four days we explore DC,
traveling between museums and memorials,
the National Mall and our hotel in Arlington.
By day two we call ourselves Metro Masters,
having quickly figured out how to refill our fare cards
and navigate terminals, though I'm still not used to
the stations' escalators, so vertical
riders seem to slant backward
as they're ferried underground.

On the train I look around our car too much
to be anything but tourist, memorize the names
of each station we stop at: Foggy Bottom, Dupont Circle,
Farragut West. I fall in love with the way people hop on
and off like it's nothing, sleep during their commute
even as the constant jolts of the train rock me in my seat.

On our last day the red line is stopped,
a service alert flashing the reason on a marquee
above the escalators: *person struck at Columbia Heights.*
No one else waiting seems alarmed, not the children
and their parents, the sightseers, the other couples like us,
not the occasional panhandler roaming
from person to person with his plastic cup
calling out *forty cents, got forty cents, god is good.*

The red lights along the station floor begin to pulse
and I lean forward to see the train emerge from the tunnel,
its glaring beams, rush of air that pulls my hair
away from my face, the shriek as it slows,
a sound I thought we'd grown used to.

When I Die

Bury me with kettle-cooked chips, barbecued chicken,
cinnamon buns and snickerdoodle cookies, chocolate-covered
strawberries, beignets. Line my coffin in bumper stickers

that say "sleep is a symptom of caffeine deprivation"
and "I'm knot into yoga." Shroud my limbs
with concert tickets and arcade tokens, obols
to pay my ferry fee. Leave me shoeless

and braless, but paint my toenails some shade
of pink, maybe "Pink-ing of You" or "Kiss On My Tulips,"
seal my mouth with scratch-n-sniff stickers

so my soul can't escape. Embalm my corpse
with coffee—black—daiquiris, pina coladas,
the sweetest moscato wine. I want a shrine

like Marie Laveau's, the Voodoo Queen of New Orleans,
cluttered with offerings of used-up lighters, hotel key cards,
expired coupons, crumpled receipts,
rotting pumpkins. Have an open bar at my funeral

and have Harlequin romance novels sent
in lieu of flowers. Bury those with me, too.
My mother always told me to make sure
I had something to read in case I had to wait a while.

Herbal Lore

Ancient Greeks believed roses were red
from the blood of Aphrodite, who pricked her foot
on a thorn trying to save her beloved Adonis.
I read this on the back of an Herbal Essences
shampoo bottle, a brand I remember
for its 90s commercials featuring a woman
having an orgasmic experience
while washing her hair. At eight,
I thought all sex happened in the shower.

During your first trip to see me, we study the Greek busts
at the local art museum, comparing their half-bodies
to our whole ones. Decapitated, some with amputated limbs,
the only similarities we can find are in breasts
and lower backs, torso length and hip width. Full statues

of Aphrodite and Adonis are placed against opposite walls,
lovers flirting across the room. Unashamed of her body, her curves
encased in pale marble, she is as beautiful as she's supposed to be
while he, nose slightly bent and too thin, spine bowed in standing,
is not the god I had imagined after all.

We carefully plan out our visits so that we're never apart
for more than two weekends in a row, something we've gotten good at
after a year of long distance. It seems that it's more often now
I ask if you think you'll move here eventually, soon, ever,
so that we can be together full-time. I should know
that you're too nice to say anything less than maybe.

Myth says Adonis spent two-thirds of his time with Aphrodite,
the remaining third with another goddess, as though this slight surplus
of hours proved a greater love. Faced with a man that wasn't all hers,
I wonder if Aphrodite told him that being together for the majority
of the time does not make up for what goes missing.

Red Vines

I brush twice before bed. The first time
as routine, the second after eating Red Vines.

On a diet of water and black coffee,
I brush my teeth constantly: after eating

something I shouldn't have, to keep
from snacking, to mask with mint the acids

of an empty stomach coating
my tongue. Standing at my kitchen sink,

I try not to notice the nutrition facts
on the bag, but I remember the cost

of all my favorite things. One twist
is one-fourth the serving size, is one more

mile I'll have to run on the treadmill. Four
is too many, four twists means no

dinner. I throw the empty licorice bag
into the trash and walk to the bathroom

to scrape the color from my candied tongue.

The Fall

I.

Our pastor talks about cherubim on Easter
Sunday. Cherubim, you say, like little angel
babies, like cupid with his arrows, like paintings
by Michaelangelo. When we look it up,
we find out that cherubim guard
the gates of Eden, protecting
paradise from you and me.

II.

The condom breaks. Thin
latex stretches, shatters
statistics: *97 percent effective when used
properly*. We should have stuck to the variety
pack of twelve, but the box claimed these
were as close to skin as we would come.

III.

That night I dream of babies
with four faces, beaks shrieking
as they swoop from the sky to swallow
me, their lion's manes tangled
with flames, their flapping wings covered
in hundreds of unblinking eyes.

A Failing Heart

Say an extra prayer
or two, my mother tells me,
but I haven't threaded my fingers
since the nights I knelt beside the bunk beds
shared with my sister.

I recite the words now, anyway.
I'm afraid if I don't,
these constant machine beeps
will be the last sound you hear.
If I don't,
my mother will never stop mumbling,
no news is good news, no news is good news,
a half-believed mantra guiding her pilgrimage
from vacant room to vacant room.

I can still hear the way we would giggle
on your front porch,
decorated with crinkled feather boas
and plates of crumbled Neapolitan wafers,
your gray hair tucked under a wide brim
of netted straw,
your magnified eyes peering over
the edge of a miniature cup
whose handle was made for pinkies
much smaller than yours.

Bare gums and smacking lips,
you sang of a flightless yellow bird.

The Summer Solstice

*On June 21, 1333, Petrarch watched
the women at Cologne rinse their hands and arms
in the Rhine so that the threatening calamities of the
coming year might be washed away
by bathing in the river.*

I. 3 PM

This tin-roofed house hums with heat
and we draw the blinds tight
against the Midsummer sun,
slather ourselves with cooling aloe gel,
take our coffee black and with ice.

II. 4 PM

Remember the ABCs of melanoma,
my dermatologist says. *Check your moles
for asymmetry, irregular borders and colors,
a large diameter. I see freckles here
on your chest, do you use sunscreen?
Most women develop cancer
in this area first.*

III. 6 PM

Carcinogens are everywhere. Studies show
that men who carry their cell phones
in their front pants pockets
run a higher risk of sterility and cancer.

I think I might be pregnant. I lie
on my back with my phone low on my belly,
buy sushi, charred burgers, and deli meat,
research spontaneous combustion
and termination services, finding only websites
for local pest control. I almost call anyway.

Confession of a Heliophiliac 20

IV. 10 PM

We eat dinner late, out of forgetfulness
or bad timing, settle for fast food
from paper bags, Happy Meals
that come with gender specific children's toys
and broken animal crackers: one-limbed
lions, halved hippos, tail-less monkeys,
giraffes missing their spots and necks.

V. Noon

I go to the beach to sweat out
the toxins inside me, to sear off
all my freckles, to see how long it takes
to turn into sand. I kneel at the shore
and let the water lap around my shins
as I slowly dip each of my fingers
into the sea.

The Wandering Womb

If I lived in the sixteenth century,
I would be afflicted by headaches,
paleness, sorrow, loss of appetite,
sleeplessness, lust,
a wandering womb, which is to say
my uterus would be walking around
in the dark of my insides, bumping
into my kidneys, cursing
the placement of my spleen. I would suffer
from it, this love melancholy, an imbalance
of the humors, an excess of black bile,
a deficit of the sanguine. The doctors would
prescribe marriage, to alleviate my pains,
pregnancy, to put my womb back
in its place. But I'd rather leave
my uterus to its roaming for a while,
let it find a new place to settle, not in the center
as it should be, but maybe a little higher,
bundled beneath my lungs, a little to the left.

I Remember

after Anne Sexton

By the first of April
the brazen lovebugs began
to mate and the sunsets were
as loud as fireworks and were
as colorful as jelly beans and
we had worn our limbs
bare since the eleventh
of February and there were times
we forgot we owned clocks
and some mid-week afternoons
we took our tea with boba,
black tapioca balls bobbing
on the surface and
one day I tied my wishes
to the branches of a weeping
willow and you said
that I was your little
moonbeam and what
I remember best is that
the hand I was holding was
your hand holding mine.

Pumpkin Carving

The insides are the criss-crossed strings
of cat's cradle, and we plunge our hands into them.

This part always reminds me of birth:
our forearms deep inside, feeling
for flesh coated in slime, the strands
that attach it to the thick wall as if struggling to keep
it there, where it has been forming for months.

We spoon out the seeds that started it all,
line them on a parchment covered cookie sheet
to bake so they're crunchy, salted, cracked

between our teeth. We hollow the body out,
until it's empty and spent, scrape away the skin
to thin a spot for the face, stencil triangle eyes
and a nose, a mouth rounded in surprise,
a permanent scream.

Tornado Warning

All morning, I watched the clouds
from the brittle window in my third-floor studio,
the way they broke apart and came back together
quicker than I could keep track of, the sky lightening
and growing dim again, like drapes drawn then pushed aside.
I have no experience with weather like this, know only rain
that lasts for days, more inches in a month
than most cities get in a year, the predictability
of tropical storms and hurricanes
with old fashioned names like Edna, Opal, Fran.

So when a siren sounded from down the street,
a recording warning those outside to seek shelter immediately,
I panicked, piled possessions from closets and corners
in the center of the Persian rug I got half-off
because the fringe was stained pink.
Evil eyes, miniature wooden giraffes, black and white caricatures
rolled up with rubber bands were collected,
shoved into cloth grocery sacks alongside SmartWater
and freckled bananas, coffee creamer, frozen Bagel Bites,
two slices of seedless rye bread,
a near empty bottle of flat Diet Pepsi,

carried down to the basement where I sat
with the communal washers and dryers. I waited
for the train-like roar, for the still air outside to birth a yellow-green funnel
that would pick up the things I had left behind, carry them miles away
and drop them in someone's backyard swimming pool.
Other tenants came, not to hunker down with me
in one of three blue plastic chairs lining the innermost wall,
but to transfer their loads of wash, to fluff and fold and lament
the existence of the fitted sheet. I waited for an all-clear signal
before re-emerging, before returning to my apartment
to survey the damage done: my pantry shelves ransacked,
Yukon Gold potatoes rolling from their plastic bag across the kitchen floor.

Outside St. John's Funeral Home

I sat on the hilltop
in a borrowed dress.
I hadn't anticipated needing black
but nine year old girls rarely do.

Printed with tiny flowers that seemed too bright,
it was my cousin's,
just big enough that the sleeves left
my fingertips in their wake.

She sat with me then,
her two brothers on either side,
solid bookends keeping us
from sliding off the edge.

We didn't have slopes like this in Sarasota,
grassy angles to perch ourselves on
and chuck pebbles at the infrequent cars
passing below.

In my undersized palms,
they were boulders.

Church

Thick and short, your fingers splay wide to cover
the better part of my thigh, my left ribcage, the small
of my back. You compare them to pug puppies, smushed
and fat, say they belong on the hands of hobbits, blame them
for cramped handwriting and misdialed phone numbers.

Sometimes your fingers remind me of my grandfather's,
his that would patiently dole out taupe-colored pills for blood pressure,
cholesterol, clotting, dropping them on top of one another
seven times into blue plastic compartments. When I was younger,
he would fold his hands together, keeping his pointer fingers straight up
and pressed against each other to create a steeple,
before twisting his wrists skyward to reveal fingers interlocked
and wriggling, the people inside his church of hands.
I show you this during our third month of dating,
but you're not Baptist or Catholic, Methodist, Lutheran,
or Presbyterian, and have no prior experience with steeples.

Your fingers have never been broken or slammed in a car door.
The tips aren't calloused from playing any stringed instrument.
When you talk, you let them curl into fists in your pockets
or romp through your hair, sweeping the strands up

past your forehead. They leave marks on my ass
for hours after we've had sex, perfect pink shadows
where they grabbed and slapped, startling the skin.
Can you imagine what we'll look like when we're old?
I ask. *Will you still want me like you do now?*
And you say yes, because we're only twenty-three
and know nothing but this wanting.

The Wandering Womb Returns

Sometimes I worry that my womb will wander
too far from where it belongs, become distracted
from its purpose, forget its loyalty to me.

It won't bring me the children who are tucked away
in the fine print of its contract, but instead will bear
polyps, HPV, abnormal cells. The doctor tells me it's nothing

to be concerned about, not quite yet. It's still early.
But they call too soon after my biopsy for it to be good
news. My sample of scraped cells shows cervicitis,

a chronic inflammation of the cervix. Online I find
cervicitis linked to words like *common* and *treatable*,
alongside *difficulty conceiving* and *infertility*. My mother's

womb wandered away in her fortieth year, returned
with nothing to show for its travels but the cancer. It's this
betrayal of the womb I fear the most, its punishment
the same as my mother's: the uterus banished
from the body, condemned to roam.

Highway 301

Words that remind me of the towns strung along this road:
podunk, Southern with a capital S, the sticks, boonies,
East Jesus Nowhere. Things I pass during the five hour drive:
The Orange Shop, boarded up for the season; gas stations
that close at eight each night, earlier on Sundays; Linda's Yard Arts,
selling giant metal roosters; the "Largest Rocking Chair in the World"
across the street from the "Largest Flea Market in the World";
a monument to the Ten Commandments, its slabs of black granite
stacked in front of the Starke County Courthouse.

Then there's the tent pitched in the first field I see ungrazed
by cattle, a blue cross looming above the hand-painted sign:
"Present a living Christ to a dying world in your town today!"
There are no people congregating outside waiting for some cue
to enter, no tables lined up or picnic blankets laid out for a potluck
afterwards—and with that sinking feeling I realize I may have
missed the revival altogether, or worse, must wait hours
for it to even begin. Or maybe it has been over for days now,
the tent waiting only to be disassembled and carried to the next town.

Still, I see the parishioners that should be inside,
sweat moistening their upper lips, dampening foreheads
and collecting in crevices of skin, between cleavage and butt cheeks.

They are rocking with eyes closed, swaying with hands upturned,
held open in front of genitals and wombs, they are convulsing
in the aisles between the wooden folding chairs, slain in the spirit,

tongues lolling, eyes rolling, they are dropping
to their knees, hands outstretched with palms pressed flat
against the heavy air, moaning Hallelujah

Hallelujah O Father O God O God of Heaven and Earth O God
$\qquad\qquad\qquad\qquad\qquad$ save us save us save us.

Home and Garden Television

All summer long I watch HGTV,
though I own neither home
nor garden. My father asks me why
I fill my head with these garbage shows,
with titles like *Renovation Raiders*,
House Hunters, *Flip or Flop* but I can't tell
if it's my penchant for planning ahead that draws me in
or the alliterative titles. I say *you know, I could tell you
how much a seamless slab of granite for your kitchen
island would cost per square foot.*

When Chelsea and Eric give me a tour
of their new home, I comment on the jetted soaker tub
in the en suite, the walk-in shower with *is that quartz?*
it's so much more elegant than the usual tile, the convenience
of the hidden storage and downstairs half-bath—
both excellent features for resale.

I advise my friends and parents to upgrade
appliances, rearrange floor plans and renovate
to increase value, all the while ignoring the holes
in the walls of the apartment I rent, the paint peeling
away from the plaster in the closet, the faucets
that never seem to stop dripping.

An entire episode of *Bath Crashers* is dedicated
to a patina finish on a steel vanity, how the silver is
treated with chemicals, heated until a gold-green
drives away all the shine. For weeks after, I see patina
over everything: the knot in the wood
of my parent's back deck, the crashing Gulf waves,
the cover of my paperback novel, the wings
of a fly I crush beneath my thumb. It glazes my forehead
when I run, coats each slice of deli meat sitting
in my fridge. It's the varnish layered onto my eyelids,
cheeks, lips, the slicks on sidewalks after every rain,
the oil puddles left in parking lots when I pull away.

Compulsive Wisher

I've spent dollars throwing pennies
into shopping mall fountains,
wasted hours' worth of minutes waiting
for the 11:11 that comes twice a day, ruined
the frosting of each birthday cake with wax
from candles relit until they're nothing

but wick. On 12/12/12 I wished on a fallen
eyelash for a tiny house with creaky floorboards,
the scent of snow, cliffside roads that would lead
us both to the same place. I've cracked more

fortune cookies than I can count, searching
for a hint of the future. Some say it's bad luck
to eat the sweet shards, but I do anyway,
break the folded mold into pieces so small
each wafer melts on my tongue,
as though wishes can come true through osmosis.

The Etruscans believed fowl were soothsayers,
and so they stroked the sacred clavicles
of each sacrificed bird, ruminating
on their wishes. Who am I to dispute
this ancient oracle, ignore what it means
when the wishbone we snap breaks evenly in half,
a sure sign that we will both receive our pleas.

My Love

When we first met
I called him Sampson,
my love with hair of dune grass
waving to his waist,
with his shoulders of challah loaves.
Now I know, too, his chest of steel wool,
of caterpillars pulling their segments
across back decks, of thunderclouds
low in the sky.
His sternum a hammock tied between trees,
his knees the whirring wheels
of grocery store shopping carts.
My love with his tears of almond extract,
with his eyes of highway exit signs,
of damp August grass.
His fingernails of window sheers,
his knuckles the rosary beads I thumb each day,
his fingers a summer rain, steady and persistent,
tapping down my spine, inner thigh, foot's arch.
My love, his laugh a hundred ocean buoys
tethered to one another,
his voice the worn t-shirts I sleep in,
freshly laundered and warm from the dryer,
held to my face on days chilled and gray.
My love, his mouth the crystal candy dish
with the lid I wasn't allowed to lift
until after dinner,
the pastel mint drops melting,
one by one,
on my tongue.

Confession of a Heliophiliac

Forgive me, I believe in tanning salons
but not in one almighty god.

It's been 365 days since I've prayed
to anything other than weather, fate,

pineapple upside down cake. I have committed sins
in most religions, beginning

with the sun tattoo above my toes
which betrays me as no

devout Catholic, but as heliophiliac.
And when asked

what the spindly rays stand for
I'd like to say Pope Paul the Fourth,

the father, son, and holy ghost,
my tongue heavy with the host,

the eighteen years of life I'd lived
before I received this ink as sacrament.

And when asked what church I attend
I would answer whichever offends

you the least, embraces all faiths,
worships coconut oil and bronzer, ocean waves,

two-piece bathing suits, salt foam,
freckles below collarbones,

whichever congregation tithes
in broken sand dollars, drives

convertibles, and celebrates solstice holidays,
Apollo, Wala, Inti, and the Eye of Ra,

sings of chariots carrying fire through the morning sky,
sings hallelujah, rub-a-dub-dub, let there be light.

About the Poet

Rochelle Germond was born and raised in Sarasota, Florida. She holds a BA in English from the University of South Florida and an MFA in Poetry from North Carolina State University. Her poems have appeared in *Hunger Mountain, Gulf Coast, The Main Street Rag, Saw Palm,* and *Split Rock Review*, among others. She teaches English at Campbell University in North Carolina, where she lives with her husband and their extensive collection of coffee mugs. This is her first chapbook.

Acknowledgements

I am deeply grateful to all of the editors of the following publications where these poems, sometimes in different form, first appeared:

Apricity Press: "Highway 301," "Hunger"
Aura Arts Literary Review: "Red Vines"
The Battered Suitcase: "A Failing Heart"
The Bitchin' Kitsch: "Playing House"
The Broken Plate: "Church," "When I Die," "Somewhere North"
Emerge Literary Journal: "The Fall," "Long Distance Relationship"
espresso ink: "Gram's House"
FLARE: The Flagler Review: "Herbal Lore"
Gulf Coast: "My Love"
Hunger Mountain: "Seasonal Affective Disorder"
The Main Street Rag: "The Wandering Womb," "Pumpkin Carving"
The Milo Review: "Missing," "Compulsive Wisher," "Things I Didn't Know I Loved"
One: "The Problem with Moving to Raleigh"
Third Wednesday: "Outside St. John's Funeral Home"
Saw Palm: "The Summer Solstice," "Confession of a Heliophiliac"
Split Rock Review: "Home and Garden Television"

Special thanks to my former teachers and workshop mates, who helped me find my voice and fine-tune many of these poems, and to James P. Cooper and Ruth J. Heflin at Choeofpleirn Press for publishing this chapbook and offering guidance along the way. I feel very lucky to have such supportive friends and family, and am especially thankful for my parents, who have loved me unconditionally; my sister, who has encouraged me always; my nephews, who provide countless moments of joy; and Jerred, who believes in me unfailingly, inspires me endlessly, and champions all of my dreams.

Jonathan Holden Poetry Chapbook Contest

First Time Poets

Submit your poetry chapbooks of 25-40 pages

By April 30, 2025

$20 entry fee

Winning poet receives $250, 10 copies of the print book, and free social media advertising

Follow our Submission Guidelines:

https://www.choeofpleirnpress.com/poetry-chapbook-contest

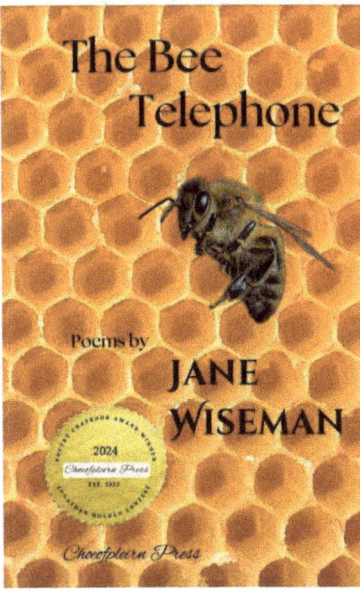

2024 Winner
Jonathan Holden Poetry
Chapbook Contest

Hosted by

Choeofpleirn Press

Imagine picking up a phone and hearing an alien voice or pressing our noses against glass to watch aliens work.

Jane Wiseman allows us to tune in to the sights and sounds of our universe, even though they may seem as alien as listening to *The Bee Telephone*.

Green Acre

Poems by

Cody Shrum

Choeofpleirn Press

1st Finalist
2024
Jonathan Holden
Poetry Chapbook Contest

Hosted by

Choeofpleirn Press

These poems are about awe, about how the simplest moments of our lives are the most important—sharing stories with family in the car or on the boat, that first kiss with a future spouse "for no reason" (which he knows is actually the best reason). Most people don't realize until much later how important these quiet moments, these "bright whispers" are, but what makes Shrum's work so extraordinary is that he understands their reverence as he lives them.

Melissa Fite Johnson,
author of *Midlife Abecedarian* and *Green*.

Listening for Low Tide

Listening
for Low Tide

Poems
James P. Cooper

Available at Amazon and
Choeofpleirn Press

Listening for Low Tide

Too much happens at ground level:
the kids selling candy or delivering
newspapers shortcut through the yard,
the neighbors' dogs blare their alarms
in unison, and teens, shielded by the heartbeat
of their music, speed down the street.

Two stories above the ground,
I welcome the afternoon sunlight
as it stretches across the rug,
my cat moving with it. From the opposite
window, the shadows cast by trees
overspread the ground, the sunlight only
hitting the treetops. Sound waves lap
against the building, the tide at its lowest
each night when the owl in the park
starts to hoot its presence.

Confession of a Heliophiliac 38

Choeofpleirn Press
www.choeofpleirnpress.com
2024

www.ingramcontent.com/pod-product-compliance
Lightning Source LLC
Chambersburg PA
CBHW051250120626
46547CB00014B/1873